TABLE OF CONTENTS

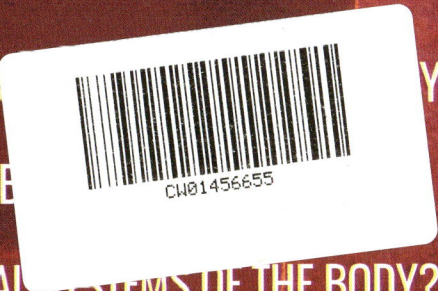

Pixa Education

CW01456655

HUMAN BODY

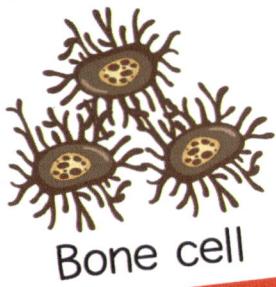

Bone cell

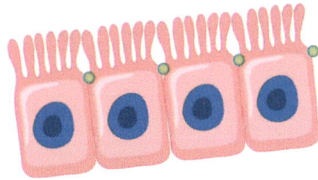

Intestinal cells

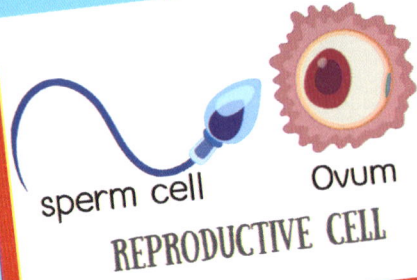

sperm cell   Ovum

REPRODUCTIVE CELL

Every second, about **20** million cells divide into two daughter cells.

A skin cell has a lifetime of 4 weeks before renewal. The lifetime of a red blood cell is about 120 days and that of a lung cell is 400 to 500 days.

Our DNA contains about 25,000 genes.

The cell is the basic unit of our body, each cell has a nucleus. This nucleus contains all our genetic information which is contained in our chromosomes which in turn contain our DNA.

Genetic information such as hair color or sex is distributed over 46 chromosomes (23 pairs of paternal origin and 23 of maternal origin).

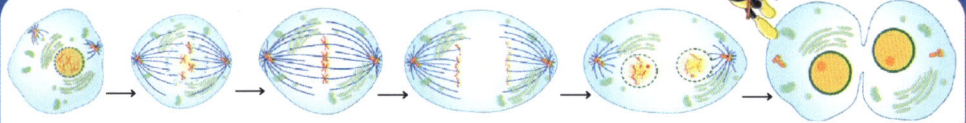

CELL MULTIPLICATION

Nucleus

Cell

Chromosome

DNA

Neurons

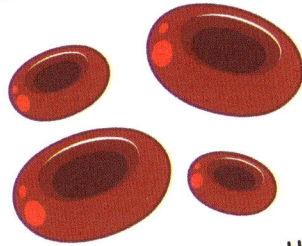

Red Blood cell

There are 100 000 billion cells. If you put them all side by side, you will get a wire of more than 15 000 km long.

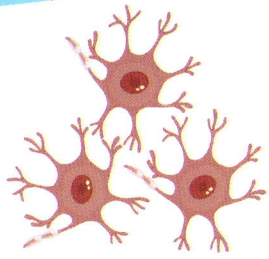

The smallest human cell is the sperm. The largest is the egg cell and the longest cells are the neurons, some of which can be more than a meter long.

ANATOMY OF THE HUMAN CELL

Cell membrane

Nucleus

Cytoplasm

Mitochondria

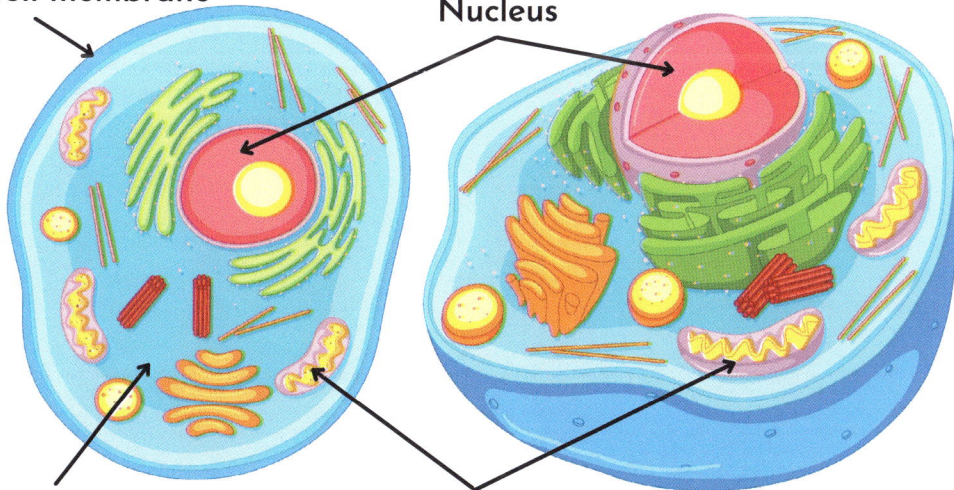

2 HOW DOES THE HUMAN BEING REPRODUCE?

- In men, the reproductive system includes both the testicles and the penis. Not very active during childhood, the testicles produce male sex cells, called sperm.

The testicles also play an endocrine role by secreting the primary male sex hormone, testosterone.

- The woman has a pair of sex glands: the ovaries. they are responsible for the production of eggs and hormones (estrogen and progesterone). they are buried deep inside the abdomen but communicate with the outside through a system of ducts and cavities including the fallopian tubes, the uterus and the vagina.

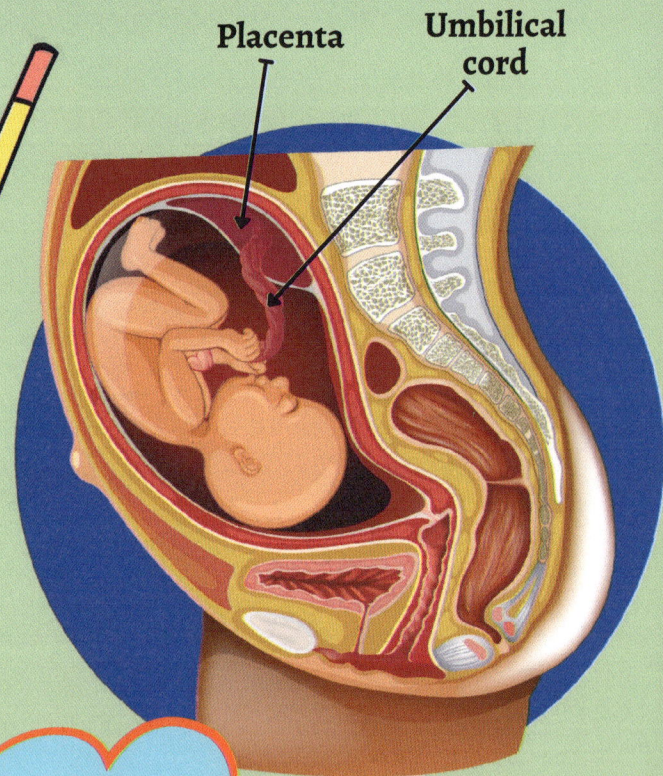

Placenta

Umbilical cord

The fetus does not breathe through the lungs, but receives oxygen and nutrients through the placenta and umbilical cord

1 Week   2 Week   4 Week   5 Week   6 Week   7 Week

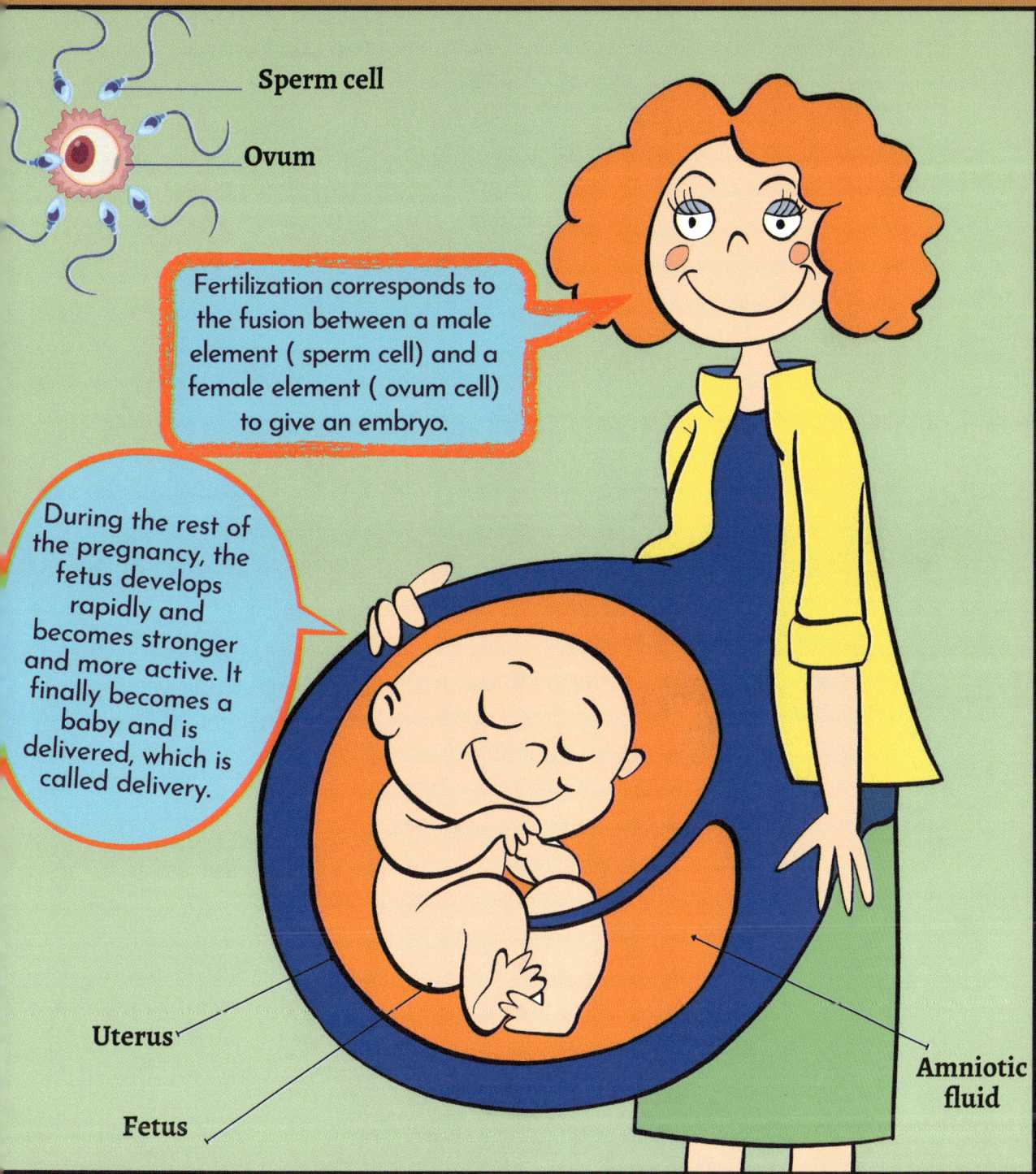

Sperm cell

Ovum

Fertilization corresponds to the fusion between a male element (sperm cell) and a female element (ovum cell) to give an embryo.

During the rest of the pregnancy, the fetus develops rapidly and becomes stronger and more active. It finally becomes a baby and is delivered, which is called delivery.

Uterus

Fetus

Amniotic fluid

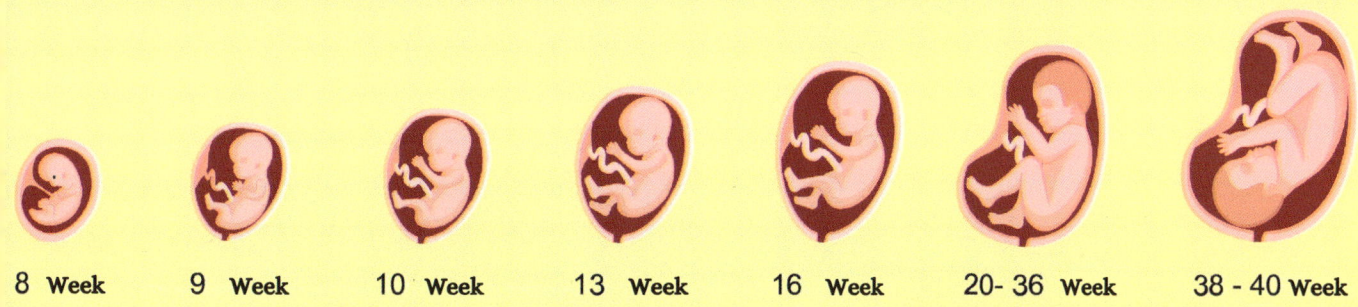

8 Week   9 Week   10 Week   13 Week   16 Week   20- 36 Week   38 - 40 Week

1- *The respiratory system*: its main organ is your lungs.

2- *The hormonal system*: it uses powerful chemicals to control your body and your mood.

3- *The immune system*: it destroys the germs that attack your body.

4- *Skin, hair and nails*: protect your body.

5- *Urinary system*: it helps to clean the blood and eliminate chemical residues.

6- *Reproductive system*: these are the organs that make your babies.

7- *Nervous system*: it carries nerve signals and commands throughout the body to control movements and reactions.

8- *Digestive system*: breaks down food to give your body energy and materials.

9- *Cardiovascular system*: transports blood and oxygen throughout the body.

10- *Muscular and skeletal system*: maintains your body's attitude and movement.

Try to identify my organs!

Anatomy is the science of studying the structure of the body of living beings, their morphology and the position of their organs.

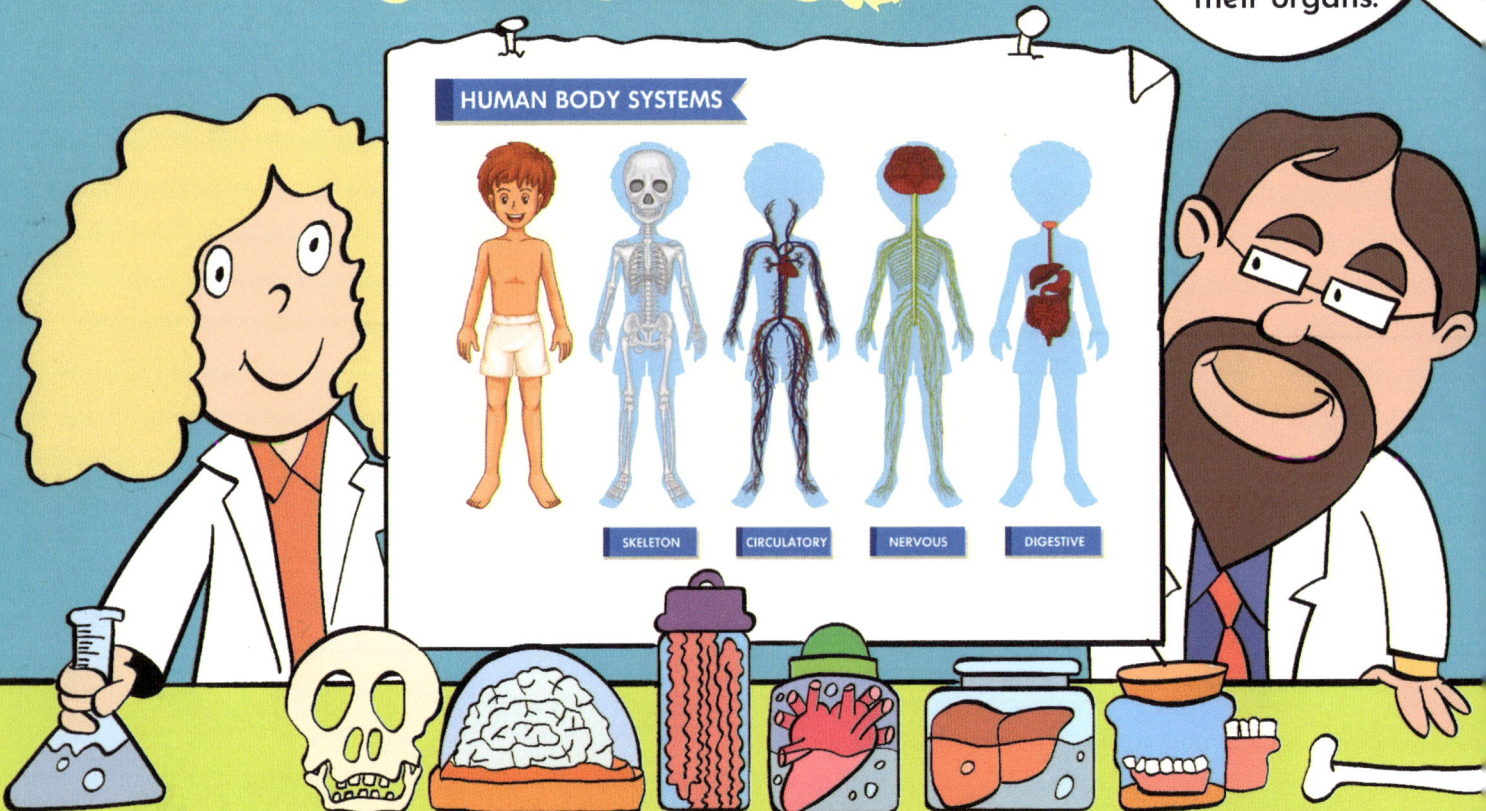

HUMAN BODY SYSTEMS

SKELETON   CIRCULATORY   NERVOUS   DIGESTIVE

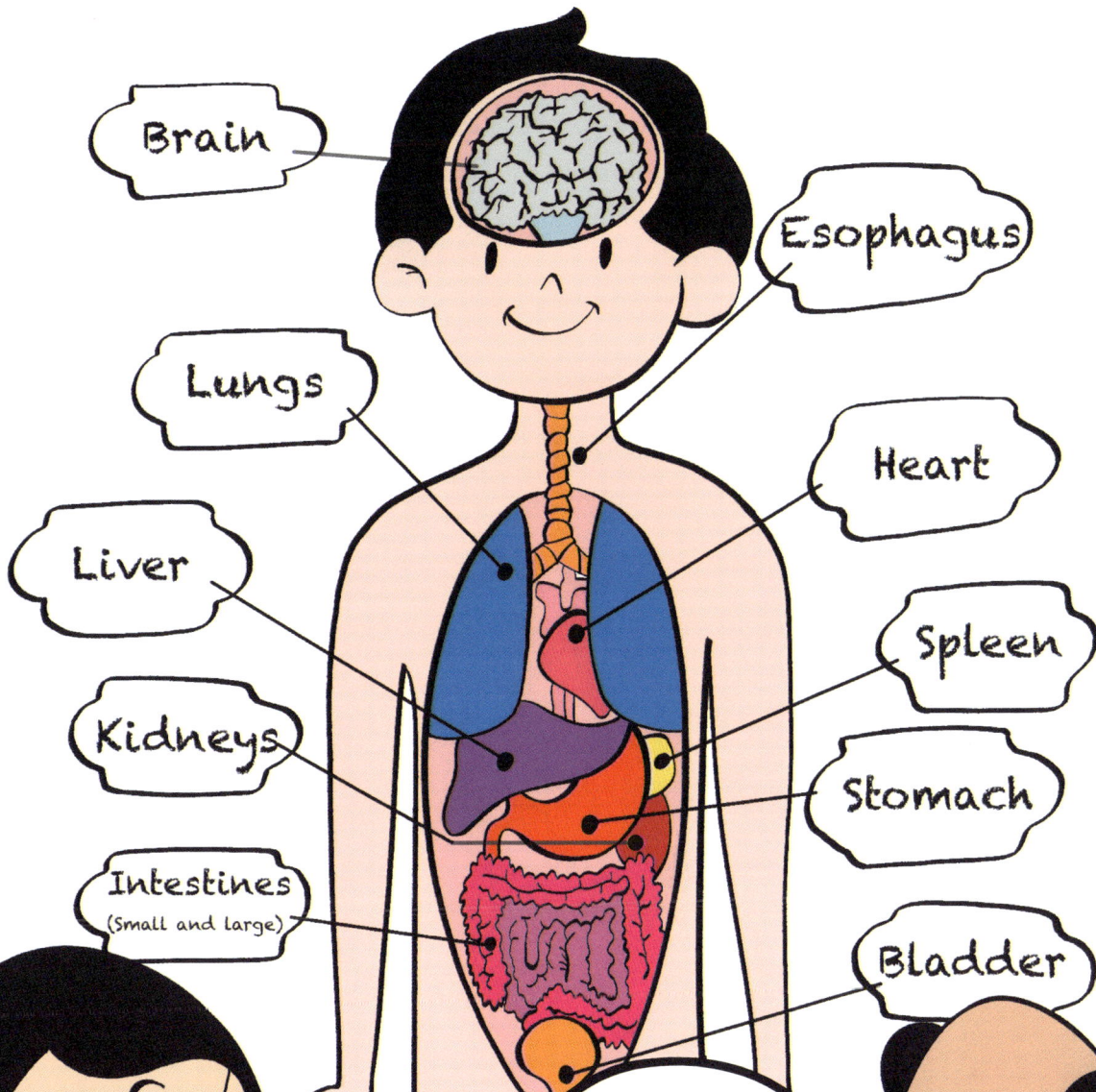

HOW IS THE HUMAN BODY ORGANISED?

4

The human body is made up of several regions, each region containing one or more organs:

- The head region: where the face, skull and jaws are located.
- The cervical region: where we find the throat, the larynx.
- The trunk: where we find the chest (thorax), the belly (abdomen), the pelvis, the genital or sexual region, the buttocks.
- The upper limbs: this is the shoulder area, the arms, the elbows, the forearms, the wrists, the palm and the back of the hand.
- The lower limbs: these are mainly the thighs, the right and left knees, the calves, the ankles, the heel, the sole and the back of the foot.

There are 6 vitcl organs: the kidneys, pancreas, liver, lungs, heart and brain. The vital organs are protected by the rib cage and the skull.

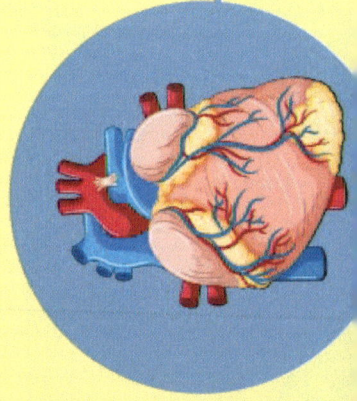

BRAIN

It ensures unconscious functions, and the proper coordination of voluntary movements and all mental functions and consciousness.

HEART

Its function is to circulate blood in the body

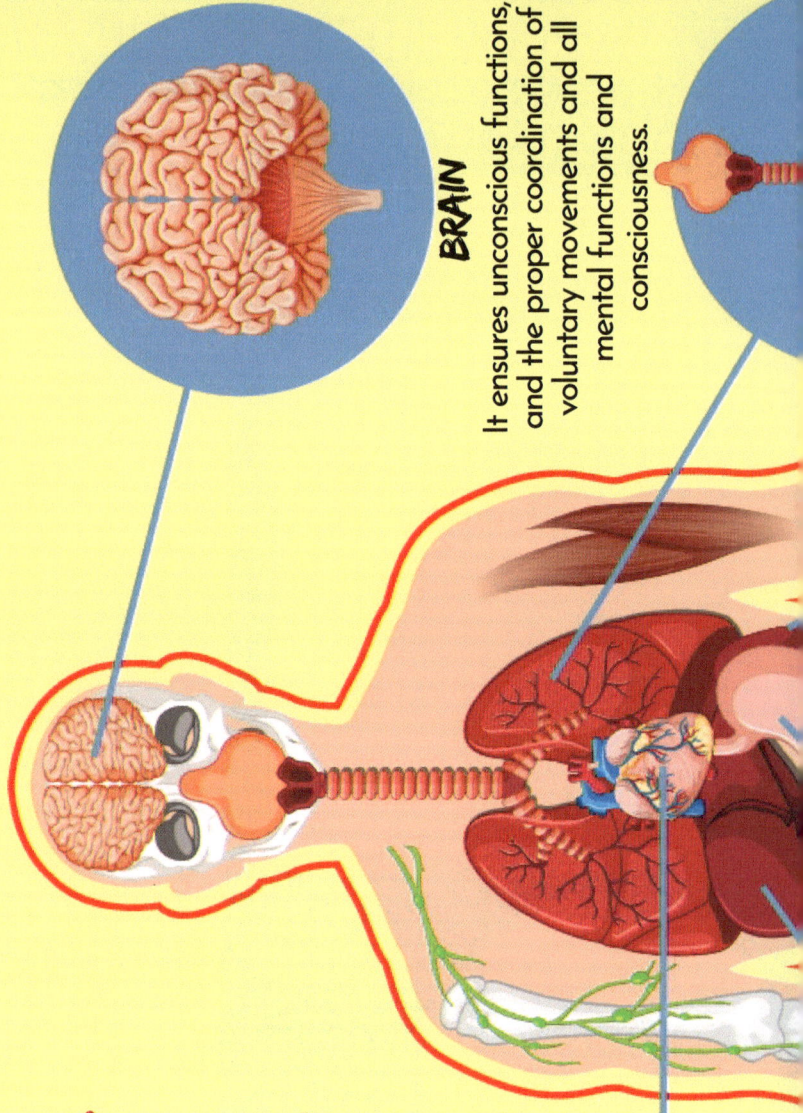

LUNG

allows gas exchange between the human body and the ambient air

SPLEEN

Involved in the maturation of red blood cells and purification of the blood.

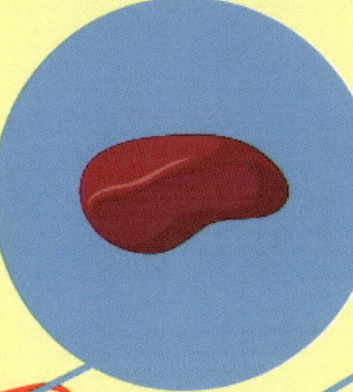

INTESTINE

Its function is to move food forward and especially to absorb nutrients.

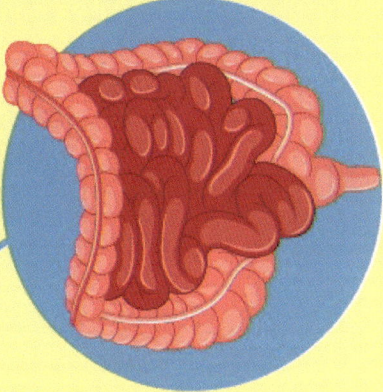

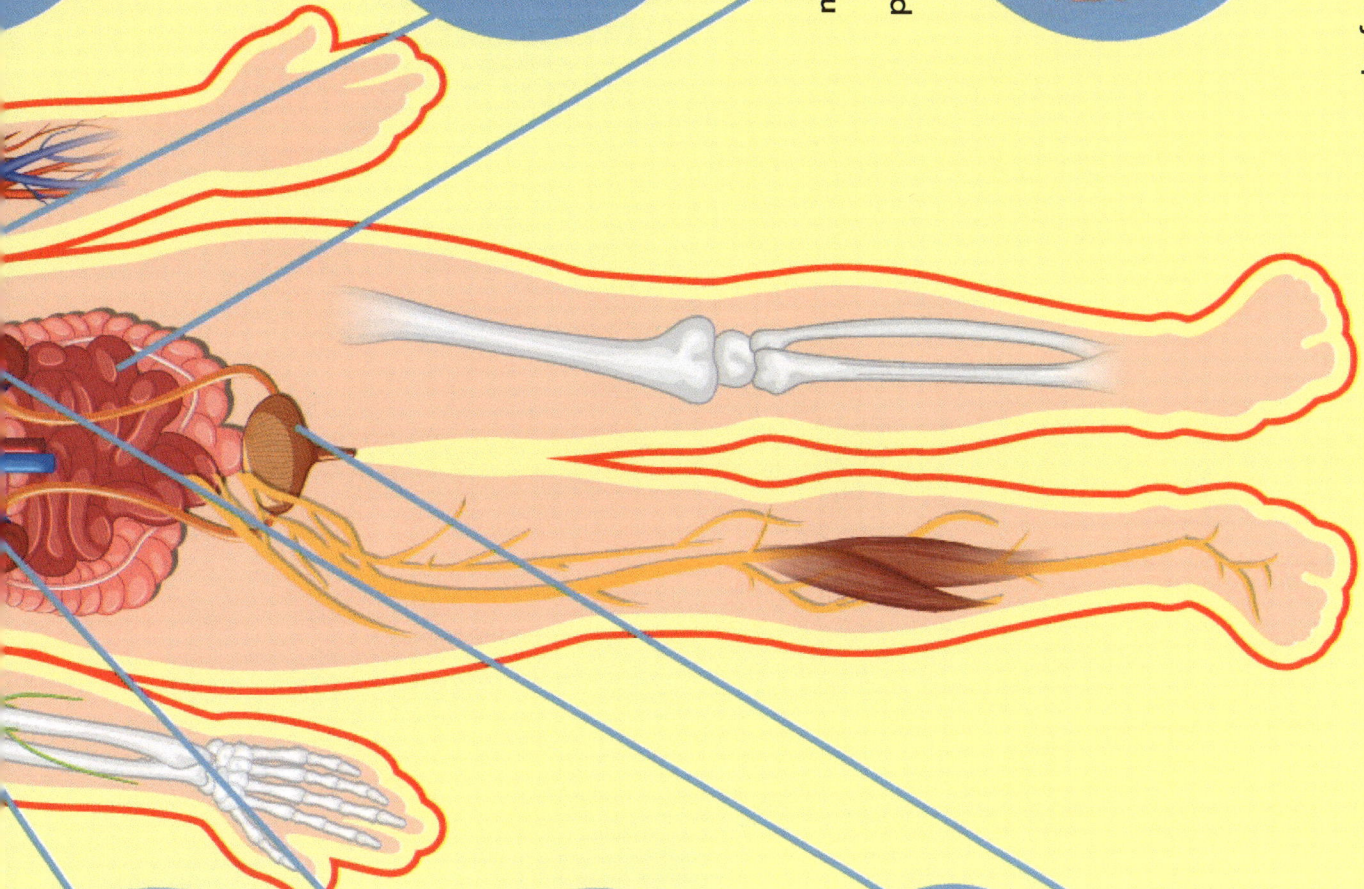

LIVER

Its functions include filtering and purifying the blood, processing and storing substances absorbed by the digestive tract.

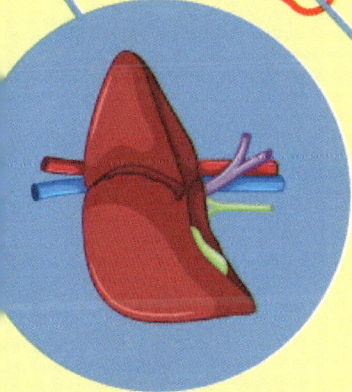

STOMACH

3 main functions: storing food, stirring it and breaking it down.

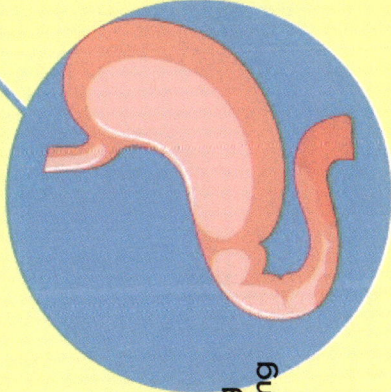

KIDNEY AND BLADDER

It produces, stores and eliminates urine, toxins and waste products after purifying the blood.

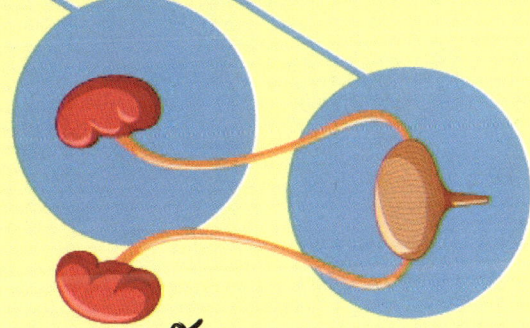

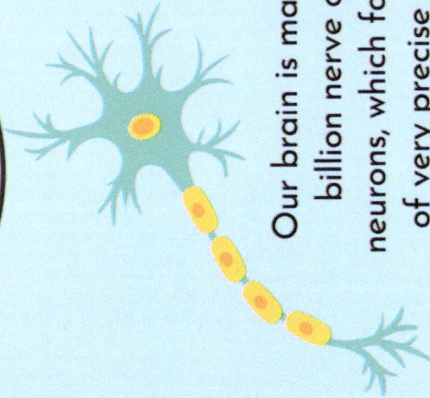

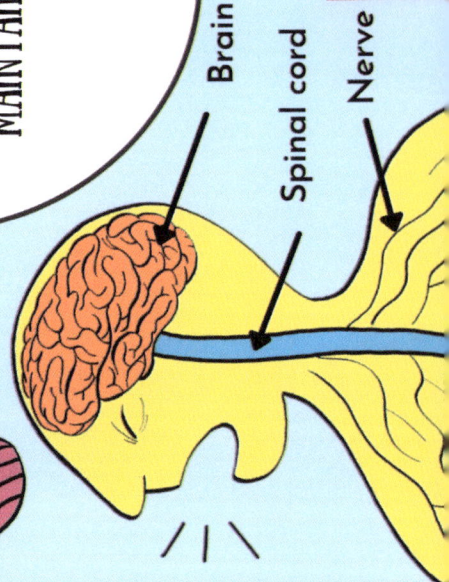

Mature neurons do not regenerate, because they are non-dividing cells.

Step 2

The spinal cord processes the information and sends a message to the motor nerves which transmit it to the muscles which then react to the stimulus.

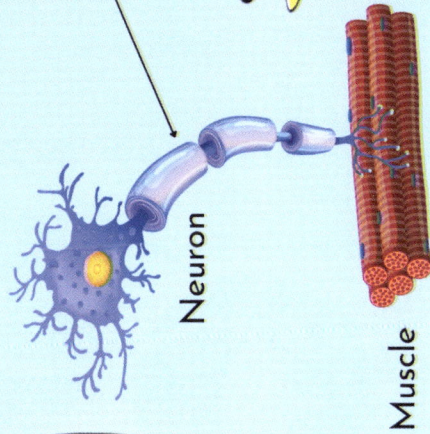

Step 1

A reflex is an involuntary and very rapid muscular response to a danger. When the latter is felt by a receptor located in a part of the body, the nerve impulse propagates on afferent fibers to the spinal cord.

Neuron

Muscle

The spinal cord and the brain form the central nervous system, capable of managing information, controlling motor skills and ensuring intellectual functions.

the brain weighs about 1.3 kg. it is protected by the skull, the cerebrospinal fluid and by 3 envelopes of the meninges.

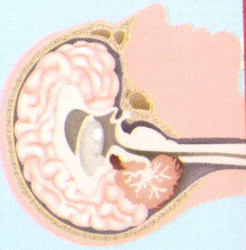

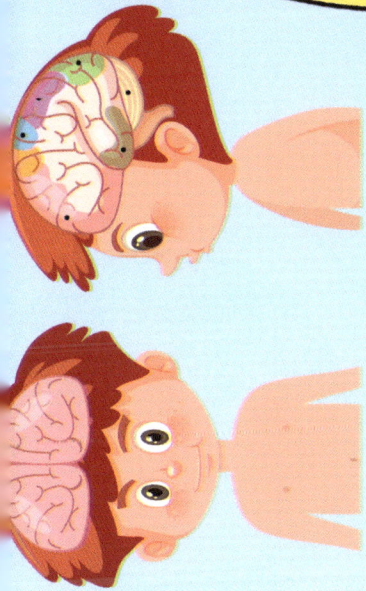

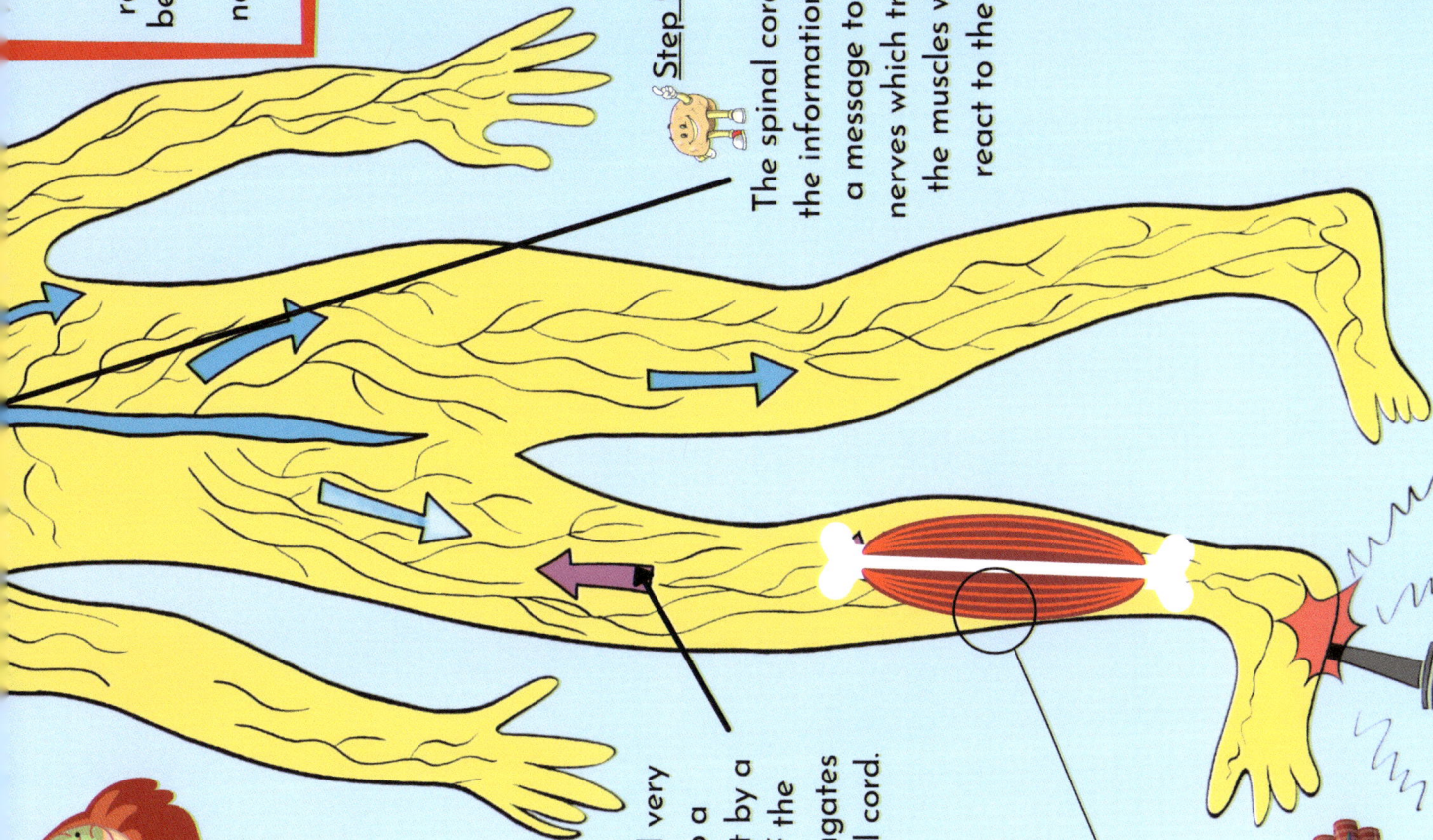

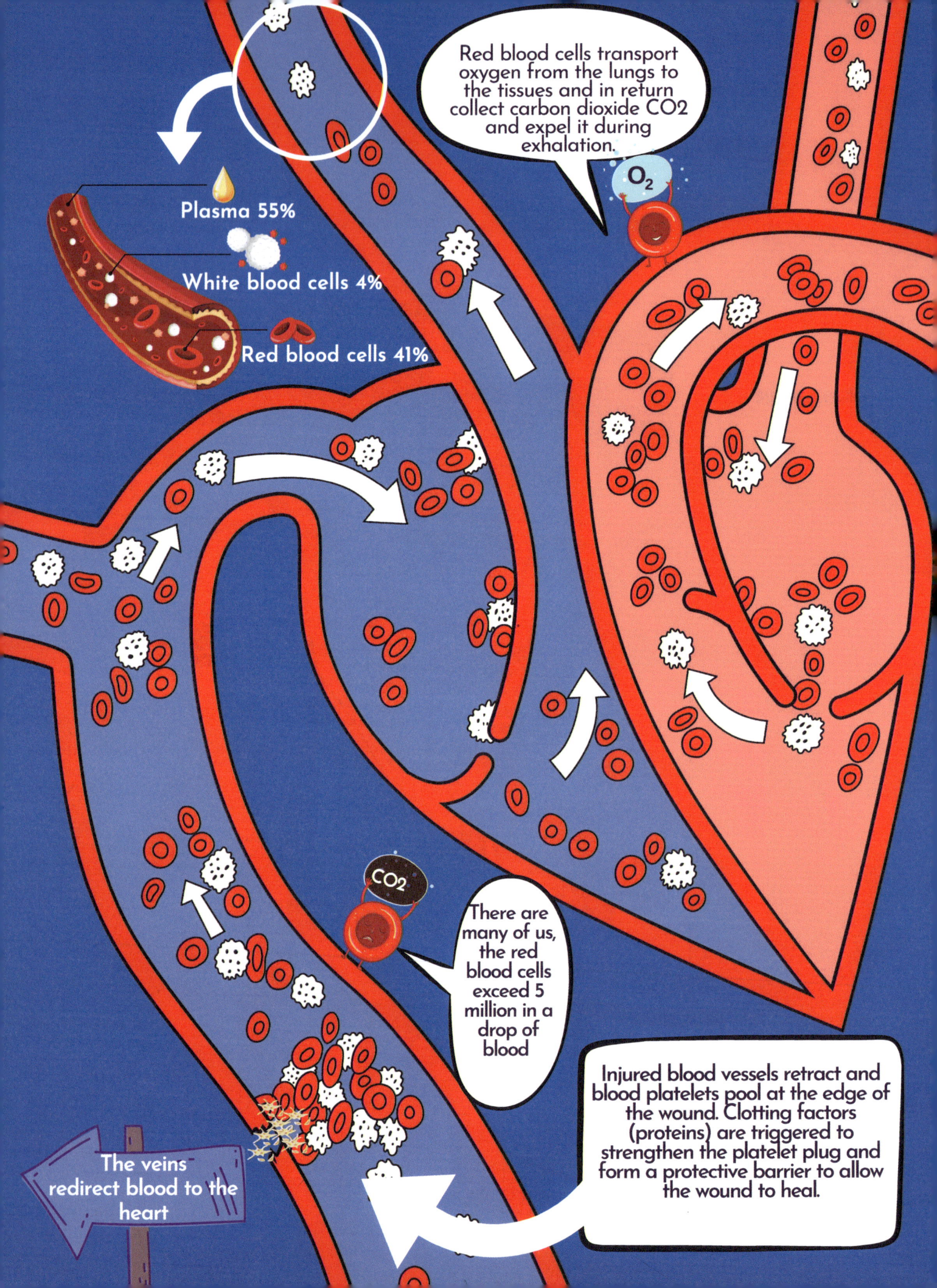

Blood travelling through the circulatory system carries nutrients, oxygen and water to the cells, starting and ending at the heart.

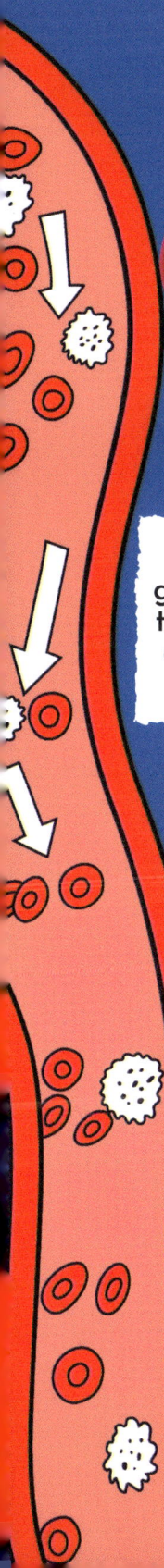

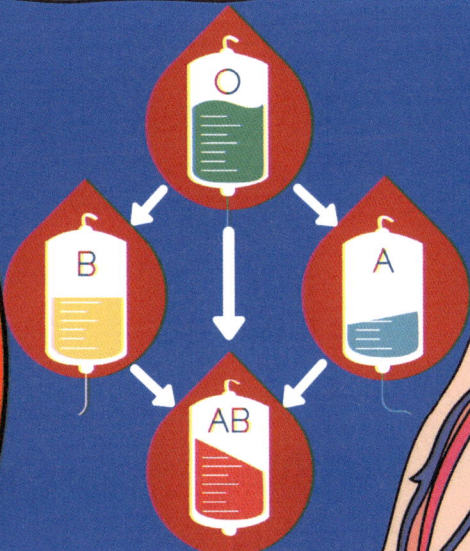

A man's body contains 6 litres of blood, a woman's 5 litres and a newborn's 3 litres.

O

B   A

AB

Individuals with group O- can donate to any recipient: they are called 'universal donors'.

In contrast, group AB+ can receive blood from all blood groups. They are known as "universal recipients".

If all the blood vessels were joined end to end, they would travel a distance of about 100 000 km. This is three times the circumference of the Earth.

Oxygenated blood leaves the heart through the arteries

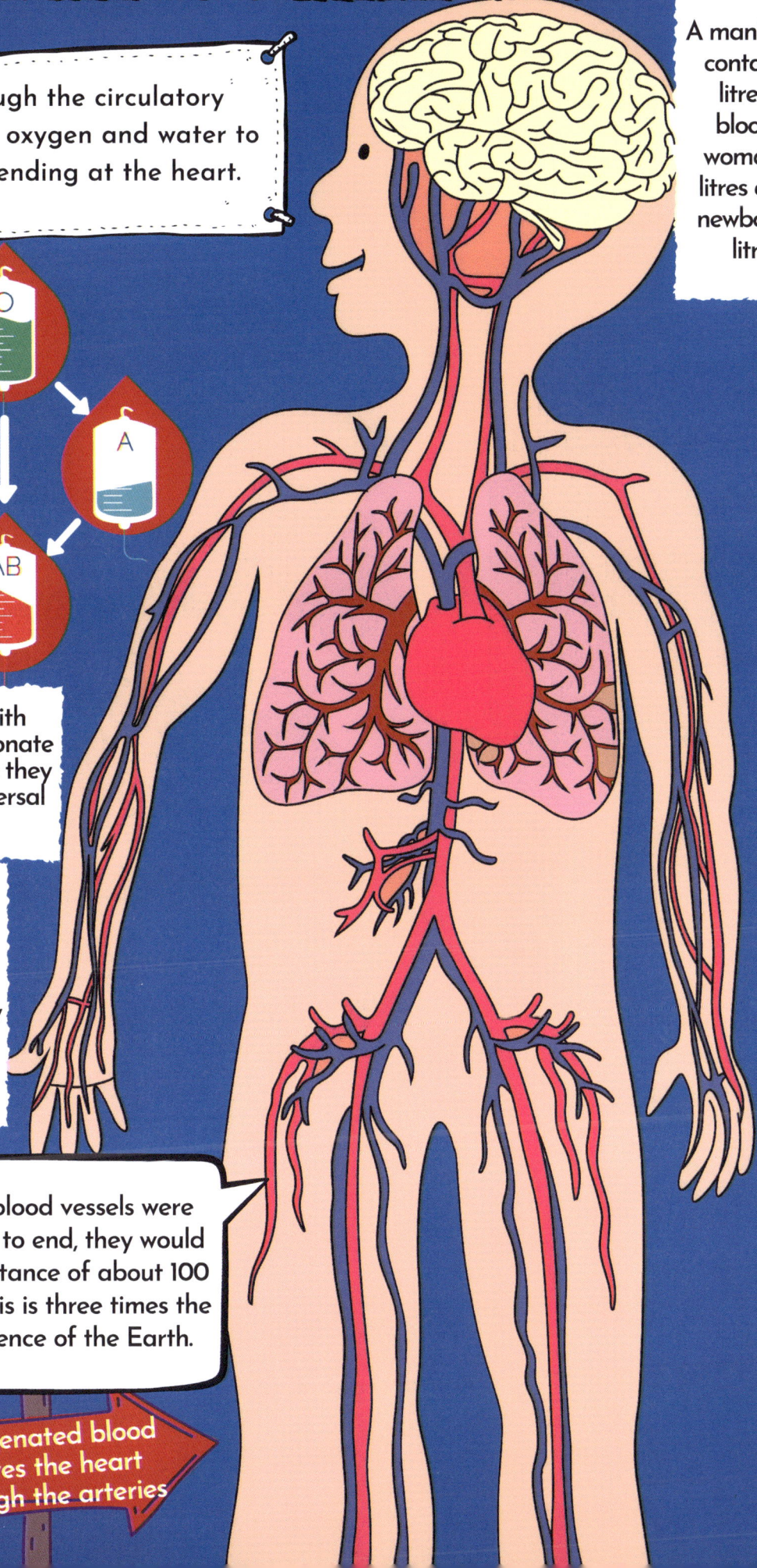

The digestive system is composed of the gastrointestinal tract, which is made up of a series of organs connected to each other by a long tube running from the mouth to the anus.

During a single meal, we produce half a teaspoon of saliva per minute.

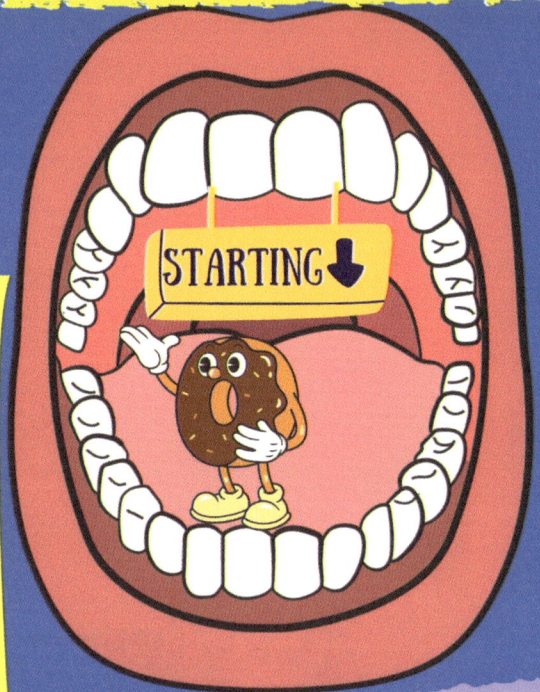

STARTING⬇

Saliva helps to compact food; the tongue pushes it to the back of the mouth, so that it can be swallowed in the oesophagus and transported to the stomach.

The muscular contractions of the stomach allow the mixing of food and gastric juice.

Saliva contains enzymes that start the chemical digestion of food.

The stomach has a double function: digestion and the progression of the food bolus towards the intestine.

The pancreas makes exocrine secretions in the duodenum (pancreatic juice) and endocrine secretions in the blood.

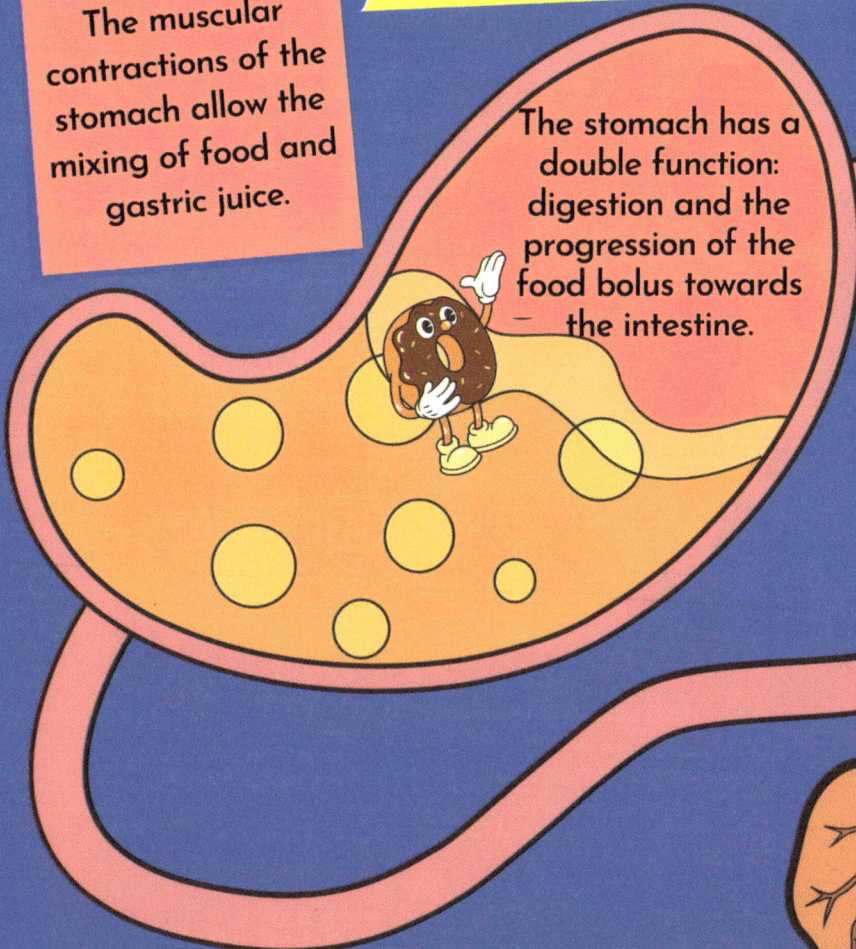

The pancreas secretes insulin into the blood to control the sugar level in the body.

Pancreas

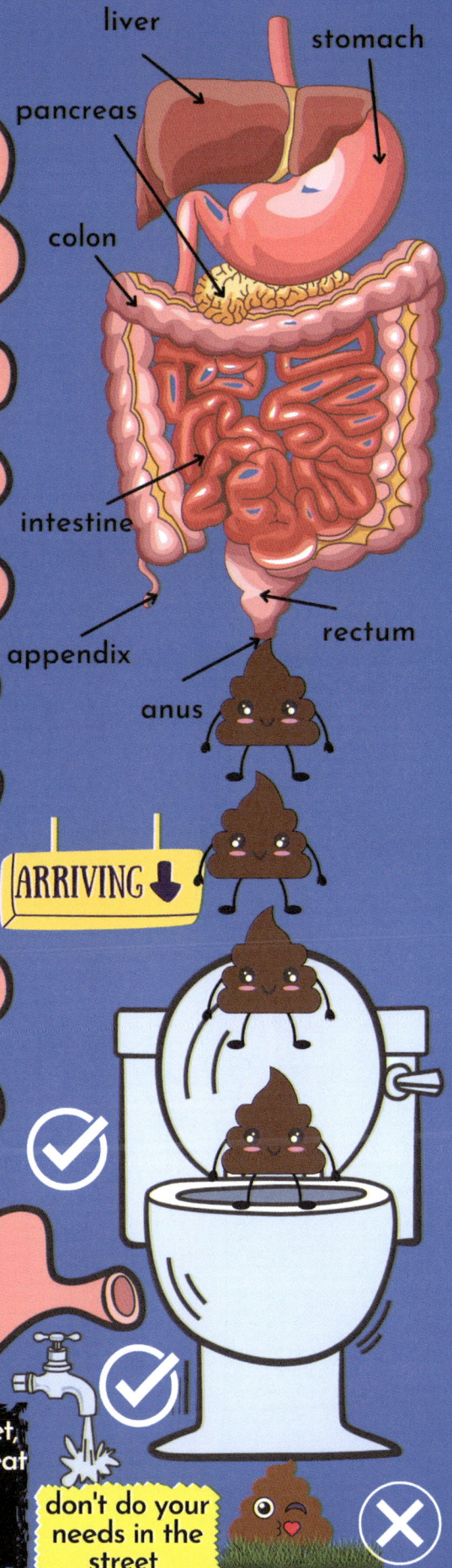

The length of the intestines can reach 3 to 6 m and its surface 200 m²

liver

stomach

pancreas

colon

intestine

appendix

rectum

anus

The role of the liver is the transformation and storage of substances absorbed by the digestive tract.

ARRIVING

the role of the colon is to collect the water that resides in non-digestible food and then to compact it in the form of stool. it measures approximately 2 metres

Tips: Eat a balanced and varied diet, eat high-fibre foods, be active and eat regularly while respecting your digestive rhythm.

Gallbladder

don't do your needs in the street

During inspiration, the powerful muscle under the lungs, called the diaphragm, descends. At the same time, the rib cage expands, the lungs expand and fill with air.

The pulmonary alveolus is a small sac-like cavity at the end of the bronchioles in which gas exchange with the blood takes place.

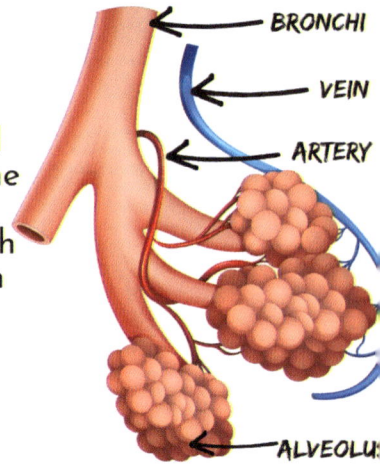

BRONCHI

VEIN

ARTERY

ALVEOLU:

Oxygen reaches the lungs through the trachea, then the pulmonary alveoli through the bronchi and bronchioles and finally the blood vessels. There, it enters the bloodstream and reaches the cells.

Asthma is a chronic inflammatory disease of the bronchi. It is manifested by breathing difficulties.

the inspiration-expiration cycle is repeated about 20,000 times a day

To protect your lungs: avoid passive smoking, wash your hands regularly, fight air pollution and exercise.

INSPIRATION

EXPIRATION

LUNG

DIAPHRAGM

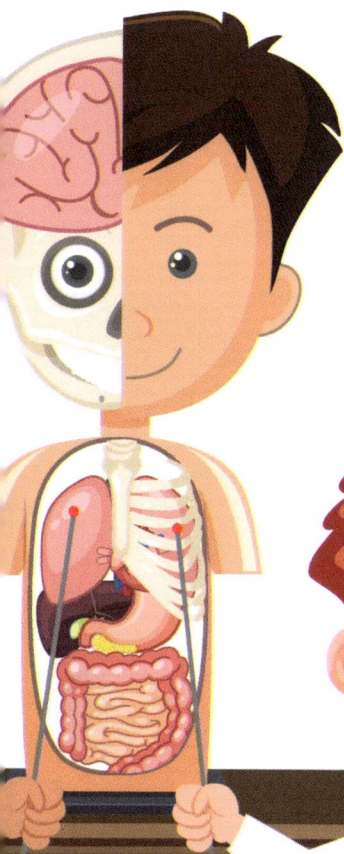

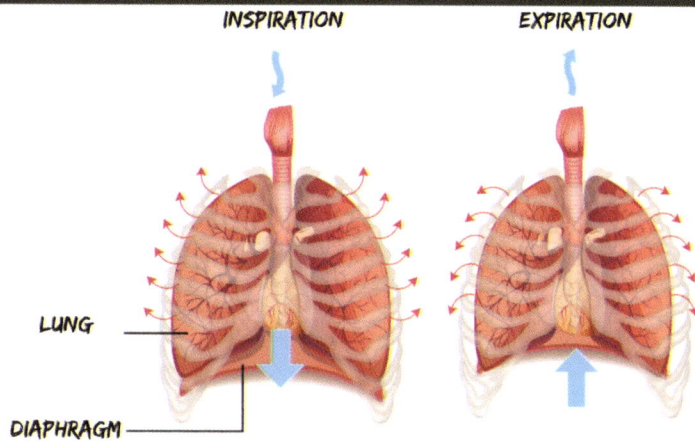

When we inhale we inhale ambient oxygen and on exhaling we release carbon dioxide.

Tobacco smoke contains over 4,000 toxic substances.

The lung belongs to the respiratory system, which also includes the airways (mouth, larynx, trachea and bronchi), the pulmonary vessels and the respiratory muscles.

In total, an 80-year-old human being will have breathed an average of more than 350 million litres of air in the course of his or her life, since an adult inhales 0.5 litres of air in one breath.

9 WHAT ARE THE FIVE SENSES?

How does the body receive external sensory information?

Information comes from the sensory organs: the eyes, ears, nose, tongue and skin. These organs receive stimuli and translate them into nerve signals that the brain can then interpret.

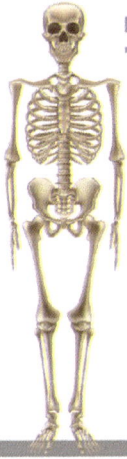

HEARING

Sound waves travelling through the air hit the eardrum of the ear and create mechanical vibrations, and the cochlea sends signals to the brain, which interprets them as sound.

OLFACTION

Chemicals in the air stimulate the olfactory cells at the top of the nasal cavity and emit signals that the brain interprets as odours.

THE VIEW

The retina converts light into nerve signals. The optic nerve transmits these signals to the brain, which interprets them to form visual images.

TASTE

The chemicals in food stimulate the taste cells in the tongue and activate nerve receptors that send signals to the brain.

TOUCH

Receptor cells in the three layers of the skin detect tactile sensations and transmit the signals to the brain, which interprets them as pain, itch, tickle or other.

The five senses allow you to know the world you live in and to make decisions accordingly. Your five senses start working in the morning, the ringing of the alarm clock, the smell of breakfast...

Cornea

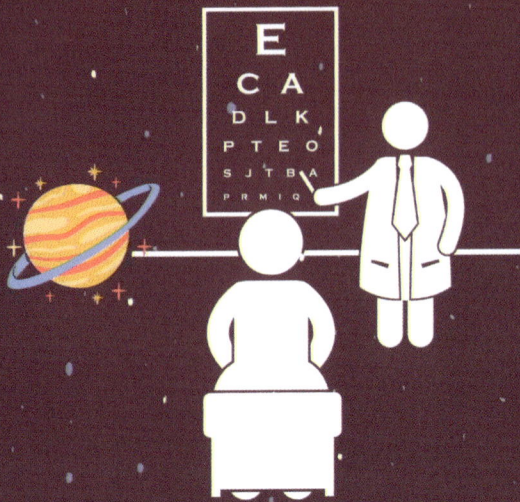

Why we blink almost 30,000 times a day: this is to 'clean' or lubricate our eyes and also to give our brain a short rest.

Hyperopia is blurred vision of a close object, in contrast to myopia which is blurred vision of a distant object.

We protect our eyes with meals rich in vitamin A such as carrots, spinach and kale, without forgetting to use good lighting and to have a medical check-up with the ophthalmologist at least every 10 years.

Our eyelashes prevent dust and foreign bodies from entering the eye. They also hold back drops of sweat and reduce sunlight.

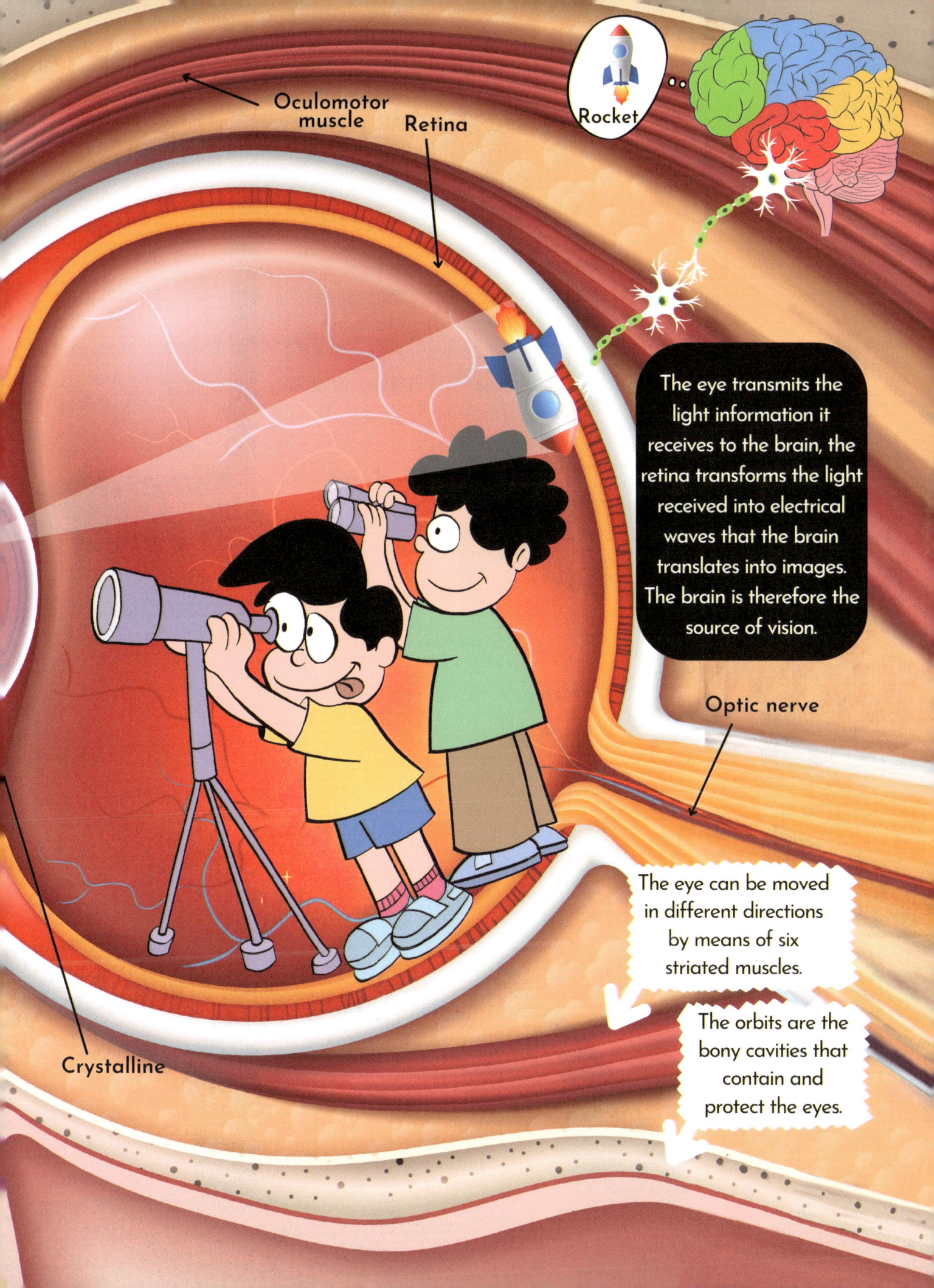

Oculomotor muscle

Retina

Rocket

The eye transmits the light information it receives to the brain, the retina transforms the light received into electrical waves that the brain translates into images. The brain is therefore the source of vision.

Optic nerve

The eye can be moved in different directions by means of six striated muscles.

The orbits are the bony cavities that contain and protect the eyes.

Crystalline

The cochlea contains fluid and sensory cells, which pick up sounds and transform them into nerve signals that are transmitted to the brain via the auditory nerve.

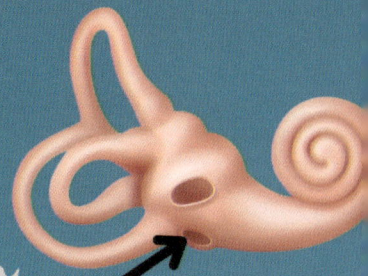

Sound is a mechanical vibration, which propagates in the form of waves. Human beings experience this vibration through the sense of hearing

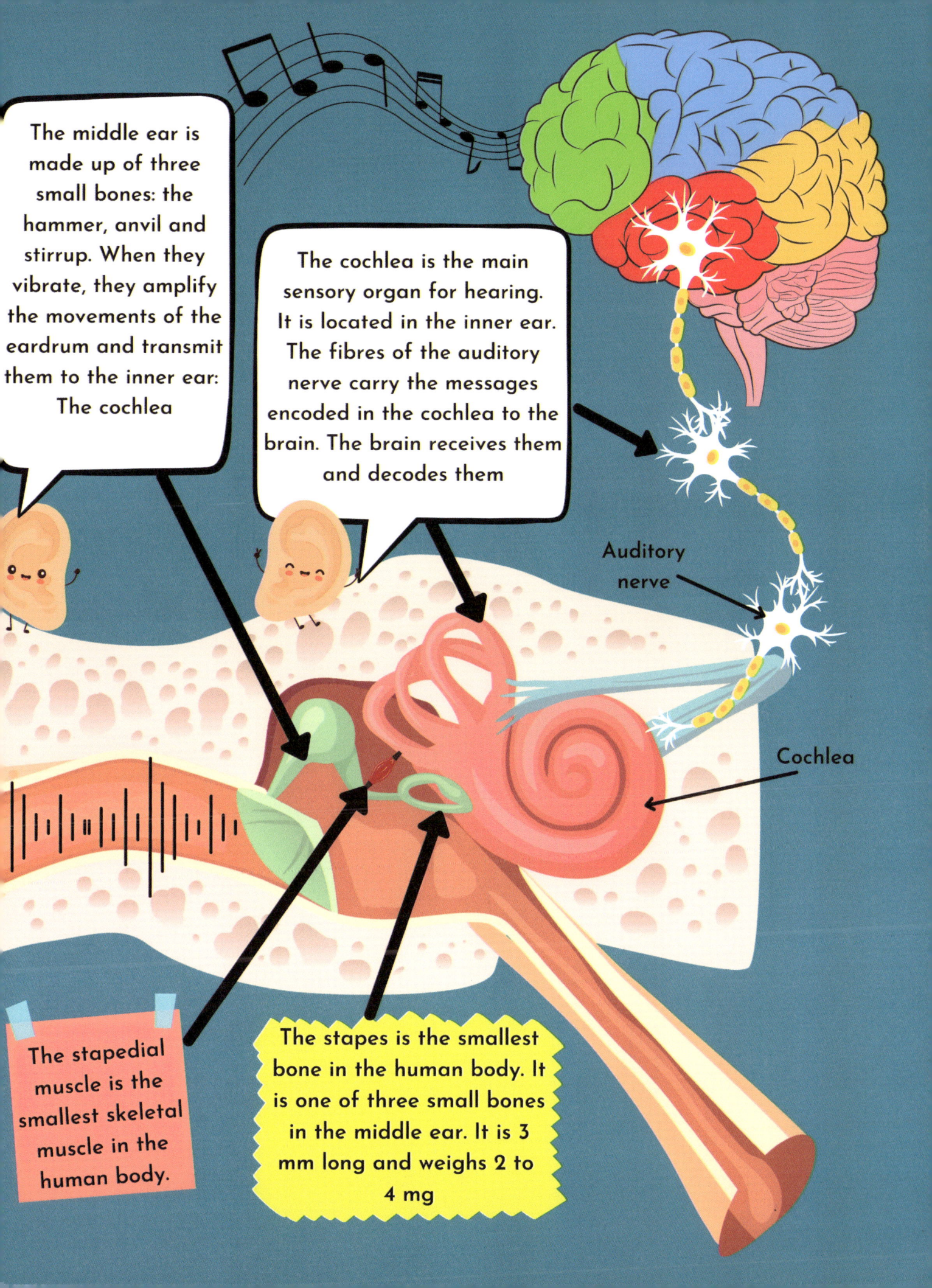

The middle ear is made up of three small bones: the hammer, anvil and stirrup. When they vibrate, they amplify the movements of the eardrum and transmit them to the inner ear: The cochlea

The cochlea is the main sensory organ for hearing. It is located in the inner ear. The fibres of the auditory nerve carry the messages encoded in the cochlea to the brain. The brain receives them and decodes them

Auditory nerve

Cochlea

The stapedial muscle is the smallest skeletal muscle in the human body.

The stapes is the smallest bone in the human body. It is one of three small bones in the middle ear. It is 3 mm long and weighs 2 to 4 mg

WHAT IS OUR SKELETON MADE OF?

The spine maintains the posture of the body and therefore the standing position, it also protects the spinal cord.

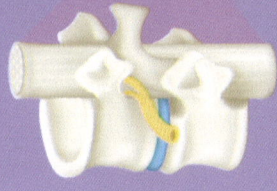

A severe fracture of the spine = a section of the spinal cord = paralysis of the lower and/or upper limbs

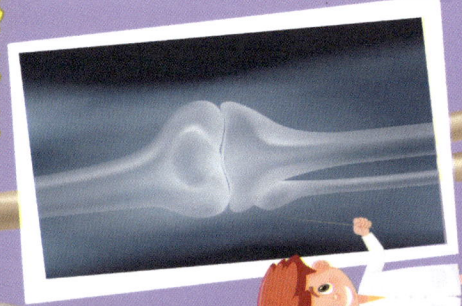

Bone x-rays are used to visualize all the bones and their joints to detect a fracture, dislocation or tumor.

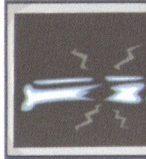

We have **206** bones

The smallest bone is the stapes (ear bone)

Bones allow you to stand and move.
They protect our vital organs like the heart and lungs.

The spine is the bone that runs from the bottom of your head to the top of your buttocks. It is composed of **33** vertebrae

Skull

Ribs

Clavicle

Humerus

Elbow

Pelvic

Radius

Ulna

Fracture healing can be achieved in 4 to 8 weeks or more and needs orthopedic or surgical treatment.

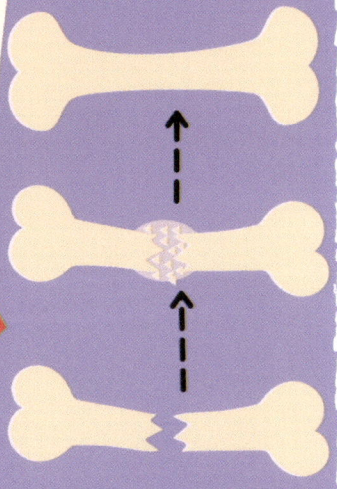

Foods that can speed up healing are: Almond, fish, milk and vegetables.

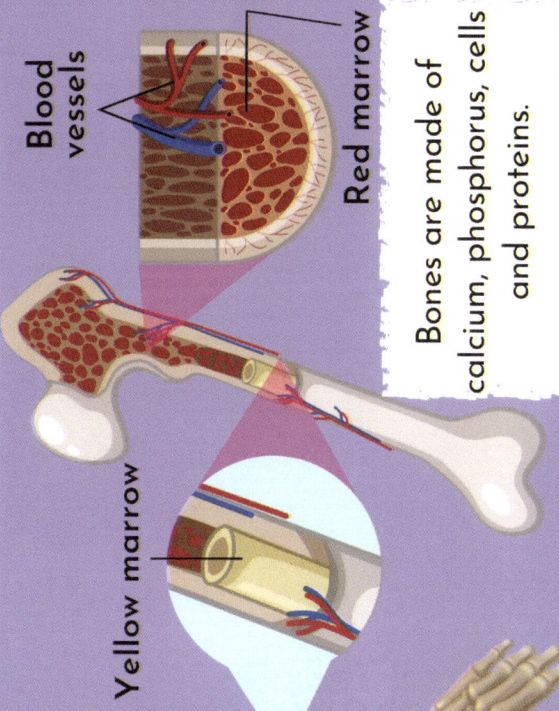

Blood vessels

Red marrow

Bones are made of calcium, phosphorus, cells and proteins.

Yellow marrow

The largest bone in the human body is the femur

Metatarsus

Femur

Patella

In 1895 the German physicist Röntgen discovered X-rays by chance.

Phalange

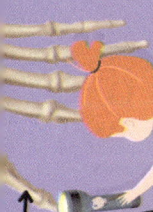

A joint is a junction between two bony ends. There are approximately 400 joints in the human body.

Muscle contraction

Flexion

The Sartorius muscle of the thigh is the longest muscle in the body, and the Stirrup muscle of the middle ear is the smallest skeletal muscle in the human body, being only 2 mm long.

In addition to regular physical activity, sufficient protein intake helps to maintain good muscle mass. Meat, fish, eggs and milk are all good sources of protein.

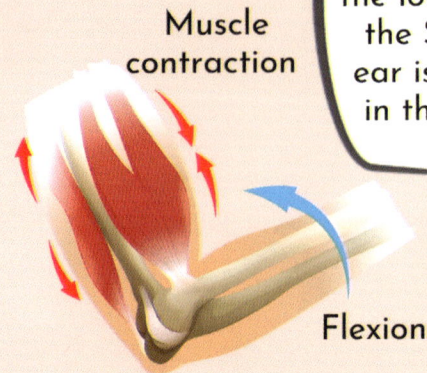

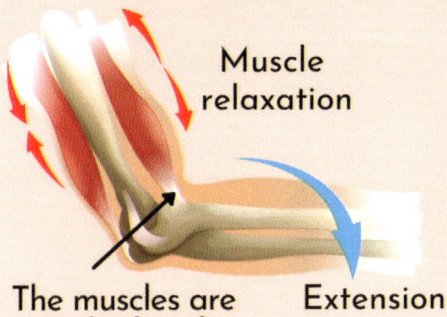

Muscle relaxation

Extension

The muscles are attached to the bones by tendons

Skeletal muscles account for almost half of our body weight.

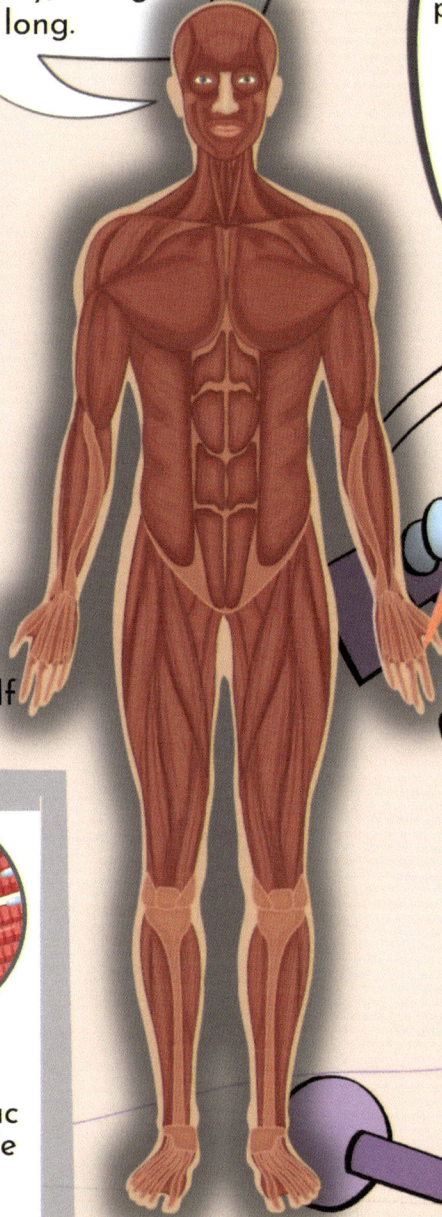

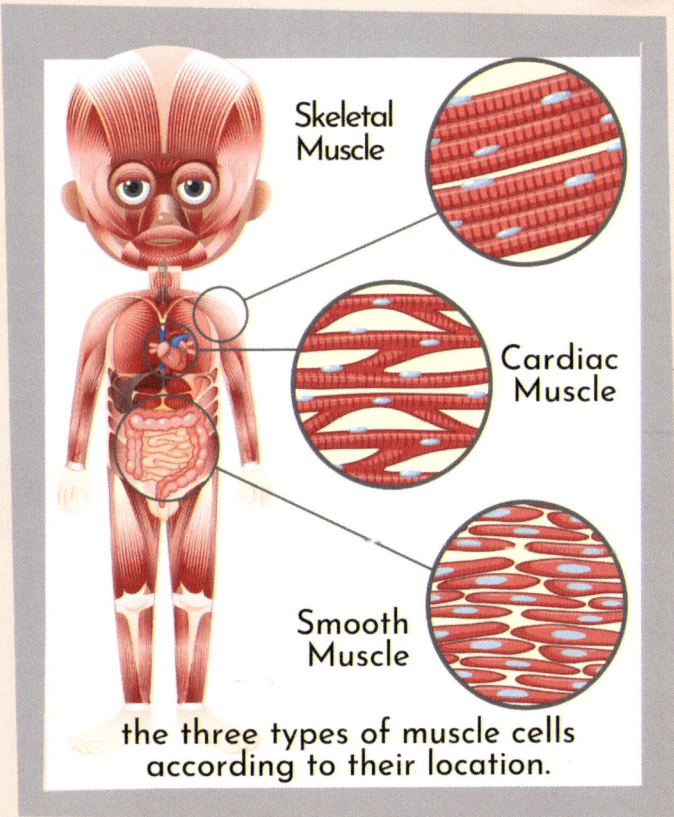

Skeletal Muscle

Cardiac Muscle

Smooth Muscle

the three types of muscle cells according to their location.

Smooth muscle and heart muscle move to ensure our bodily functions, such as heartbeat or digestion. Skeletal muscles allow us to move.

Our body is made up of more than 600 muscles.

Poliomyelitis is a severe, highly contagious infectious disease caused by a virus called "poliovirus". This virus causes irreversible paralysis. The disease can be prevented by vaccination.
The muscle is made up of thousands of muscle fibres.

Milk (temporary) teeth appear when the baby is about 6 months old. Most children have 20 milk teeth

TONSILS
The tonsils play an important role in the body's defense against viruses and bacteria by producing antibodies.

An annual visit to the dentist is indeed recommended to detect and treat certain infections and dental problems in time

The tongue plays a role in chewing and swallowing food, it is also the organ of speech and the center of taste where each region of the tongue specializes in a specific taste

A cavity is the result of a dental infection caused by bacteria that live in the mouth. They stick to the teeth in the form of plaque, which, if not regularly cleaned, can invade the walls of the teeth.

UVULA

During swallowing, the uvula closes the nasal cavity and prevents the regurgitation of food into the nasal cavity. It also regulates the movement of air in the nasal cavity.

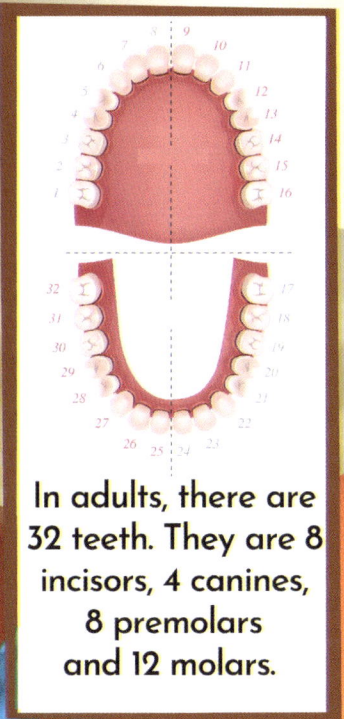

In adults, there are 32 teeth. They are 8 incisors, 4 canines, 8 premolars and 12 molars.

STOMACH

The tongue is one of the most powerful muscles in the body (it has 18 different muscles each with its own function)

Floss is used to clean between the teeth.

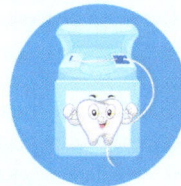

Brush your teeth at least twice a day for at least 4 minutes with a soft bristle brush

The development of cavities is caused by the sugar on which they feed and which they transform into acid.

A virus is an infectious microscopic entity that can only multiply by entering a cell and using its nucleus.

Covid-19 or coronavirus are viruses that appeared in late 2019 in China and spread rapidly around the world, mainly affecting the lung, its vaccine was developed a year later, the best way to protect yourself from this virus and most respiratory viruses are: wearing a mask, washing your hands and keeping a physical distance.

A vaccine is an injection of an antigen (attenuated or inactivated virus, bacterial membrane protein), which stimulates the immune system with a memory role to protect the patient against a future aggressor.

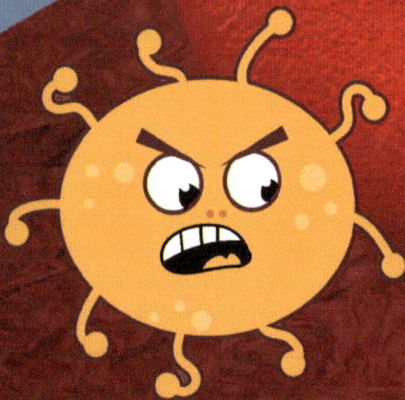

the immune system is composed of the thymus, bone marrow, spleen, tonsils, appendix and lymph nodes

Some vaccines are mandatory, such as those against diphtheria, tetanus and polio.

The first vaccine, developed by Louis Pasteur in 1885, made it possible to fight rabies.
Bacteria are living organisms composed of a single cell: bacteria are said to be unicellular.
The organism has 10 times more bacterial cells than human cells
Innate immunity allows the body to immediately defend itself against infectious agents.
Acquired immunity confers a later, but longer lasting protection.
To protect itself, the human body has two types of defense mechanisms: innate immunity and acquired immunity.

Printed in Great Britain
by Amazon